Why Be Generous?

Roland Riem

Anglican Chaplain, University of Nottingham

GROVE BOOKS LIMITED
RIDLEY HALL RD CAMBRIDGE CB3 9HU

Contents

Acknowledgements

Many people have shown me generosity in the making of this booklet. My wife Sophie, as well as being a patient reader of various versions, drew the cover picture. Revd David Runcorn found time to offer comment on the script as he prepared to move house, while Prof John Wood attended to it between exam marking and conferences. Revd Christopher Turner even took the text on holiday and claimed the risk to be worthwhile! Revd Jonathan Baker and Canon Michael Botting both blended constructive criticism with a great deal of encouragement. I am most grateful to them all for their differing contributions.

The Cover Illustration is by Sophie Hacker

First Impression August 1996
ISSN 0262-799X
ISBN 1 85174 322 7

1
The Value of Generosity

If you encourage people to define generosity, they come up with a variety of lovely ideas. Here are some from the group I asked most recently: graciousness; caring; being open; hospitality; without thought of self; listening; giving of yourself; giving freely; magnanimity. I have yet to hear a bad word said against generosity!

However, our enthusiasm for the word is not easily translated into deeds, or to be more accurate, into a generous disposition. I may be provoked into a one-off act of generosity by someone rattling a tin under my nose outside a supermarket, by seeing a particularly harrowing news item on the television or by receiving a cleverly presented mail shot—I can certainly be made to feel as guilty as the next person! But my struggle, and my hope, is to become someone who is naturally generous, a person who wants to give, who is free to give and who does give because he is big enough to give. I would like to be, but am not, a magnanimous person.

Giving for the wrong reasons may well benefit others (at least for as long as we can sustain the effort), but in the process the giver can be trapped in the snares of self-righteousness and of resenting the people or the institutions who are making demands. Worst of all, this sort of giving may cultivate a false piety towards God. Material wealth, that is our income, possessions and savings, can so easily hold Christ's disciples back from travelling along the way of their master. It brings blockages which have to be faced and overcome if we are to hear and obey his word, 'Any who want to be followers of mine must renounce self; day after day they must take up their cross, and follow me' (Luke 9.23).[1]

Wealth—the Difficulties and Defences

Even as I write I can hear myself preparing my reasons for not pursuing generosity. Like me, most readers would never think of themselves as rich. There are numerous calls on our pockets: household bills and car bills; birthday and Christmas presents; possibly a pension scheme or life assurance; the crippling one-offs, like a heavy bill from the vet or a capital item that needs replacing; and that school trip that 'everyone else is going on.' If there is any money left at the end of the month it goes towards a much needed summer holiday or an occasional treat.

This means that an exhortation to Christians to 'give what is right not what is left' may sound snappy,[2] but it fails to address the feeling people have that their budgets are already overstretched and that any further giving would mean a change in lifestyle and an unravelling of previous financial commitments. To give more many families would have to turn around and change course. No wonder

---

1 All references given in brackets in this booklet are to Luke's Gospel, unless otherwise stated.
2 The title of the course on giving by CPAS.

3

that even gentle teaching about stewardship can feel extremely threatening, as 'private' priorities and values are challenged.

Then there are those who do want to give more, who are wholeheartedly committed to the church's life, but who have divided loyalties. They may face serious trouble at home if their discipleship is expressed by giving. I know of a woman who had a violent argument with her husband when he discovered that she had been tithing her housekeeping money. Many others, and especially women who have no independent income, feel that they have no right to ask their family to make sacrifices in the name of a faith they do not share. For people like these, the call to be generous presents real practical difficulties and can lead to strong feelings of guilt.

At this point we can only briefly acknowledge the depth of the problem. We find ourselves, more or less willingly, caught up in a web of habits and responsibilities which does not make change easy. All the more reason to start with what *can* change—our awareness of the problem and our motives for doing something about it. So I ask 'Why be generous?' in the hope of bridging the gap between what we desire and how we believe things have to be, because, if we are honest, the call to generosity often feels more like a threat to our hard-won stability than like an invitation to freedom and growth.

The Power of Money

The crunch test of practical generosity is our use of money. Money is far more than a medium of exchange. It is the liquid form of our wealth. You can freeze money to turn it into possessions, or you can boil money up to turn it into various sorts of power; you can use it to impress your friends, to cherish your loved ones, to change your home, to support those in need, to guard against the proverbial rainy day. Money is also like a cushion or a wall, promising health and security. With money in your pocket you are prepared for most day-to-day eventualities and with money in the bank the world seems a kinder place to live in.

Money can be a blessing, and whatever nice people's scruples may be about admitting it too blatantly, it is crystal clear that our society knows how to put money to work. Conversely, we readily acknowledge that there has been a downside to affluence within our society, but we are less eager to admit to the detrimental effects it may be having on our own souls.[3] Of these the New Testament is also well aware: 'You cannot serve God and Mammon,' says Jesus (16.13). Mammon is an ancient Aramaic-Phoenician word for possessions or property.[4] Having an untranslated name—almost a proper name—for money in the gospel also gives a sense that money may stop being a tool and become a god which can lay a personal claim over us.[5]

---

3   Richard Foster in *Money, Sex and Power* (Hodder and Stoughton, 1985) talks of the light and dark sides of money.
4   M Hengel, *Property and Riches in the Early Church* (SCM, 1974) p 24.
5   The *NIV* translates Mammon as Money, but the capital M implies the same sense.

How money affects us will depend on the sort of people we are at heart. It would be nice to believe that our outlook was determined by our faith, but in reality our personal beliefs, convictions and values may have been formed elsewhere. Someone who has come to believe that no-one is trustable, that she is hard done by and that she only deserves the best cannot be generous. Whatever money is available will be used for protection and self-gratification. Mammon can easily find a foothold in an empty heart, and telling people to be different will not bring about change.

Starting Out on the Journey

We may well feel stuck, tempted not to attempt to tread any further down a dead-end track to an impossible ideal; but if we do persevere we have the assurance of a way forward. God offers a healthy way of living to people who have been made sick by money, which we shall be discovering in the following chapters from Luke's Gospel. The encouraging thing about Luke's 'orderly narrative' of the events of Jesus's ministry is that, while he never flinches from the ideal, Luke gives every indication that those who heed Christ's call can reach it. So we read (uniquely) in Luke's Gospel that when the first disciples were called from their boats by Jesus they left *everything* and followed him (5.11).[6] And throughout the Gospel we are introduced to men and women who step beyond even the life-giving norm of the Law (10.25-28) to draw as close as they can to the promises offered to them by Christ.

To be true to our calling, then, we also have to leave behind anything at all that holds us back (14.33). Like the rich young man in the gospel (18.18ff), we come to Jesus feeling that we really are doing enough for God, but that something is not quite right. Or maybe the sense of dis-ease is even vaguer than that, as it was for Zaccheus (19.1-10): all we know is that we want to sneak a look at the One who is passing by, and that it is worth using a little ingenuity to rise above our natural limitations and get ahead of the crowd! In either case there is an underlying sense that we lack true riches. And Jesus has a word to say to anyone who knows this, to set them on the same liberating way that he has travelled before us. If we follow, we shall discover that our wealth, far from holding us back from life, can become the very means of deepening faith and of claiming the promises of the kingdom.

Gerard Manley Hopkins, the Catholic priest and poet, wrote to his friend Robert Bridges who had lamented his own lack of faith: 'I have another counsel...I think it will be unexpected, I lay great stress on it. It is to give alms. I daresay you do indeed give alms, still I should say, Give more: I should be bold to say, Give up to the point of sensible inconvenience...the difference of mind and being between the man who finds comfort all around him unbroken unless by constraints which are none of his own seeking and the man who is pinched by his own charity is too great for forecasting. It must be felt...It changes the whole man, if anything can;

---

6 Levi leaving his tax booth does the same (5.28).

not his mind only but the will and everything.'[7]

It is good to become aware of the poverty of spirit hidden by our material wealth and determined self-sufficiency. If acknowledged, the heart's emptiness need not furnish a foothold for Mammon but can instead become the good soil in which God's word can take hold and yield a rich harvest.

Here is a quick health check for your heart:

How does my financial situation feel?

What motivates me to give what I do?

What keeps me from giving more?

7 Quoted in Donald Nicholl, *Holiness* (DLT, 1981, 96) p 102f.

2

Parables—Jesus' Weapon Against Mammon Sickness

Jesus had many different ways of confronting people with God's demands but the most characteristic of them was to speak in parables. He used them as weapons against pious people who thought that they could avoid the force of the Law. Parables are a less direct, more puzzling form of communication than straightforward commands. They are very simple stories which open up new horizons to their hearers.

Hearing a parable is like having a lens held up to an everyday world. We see at first familiar things like farmers, pearls, vineyards and kings, but the perspective is refocussed and transformed: then we catch our reflection wondering how we could fit in. Strange twists in the plot, exaggerations and paradoxes create worlds subtly different from our own which shock and kindle a listener's imagination. The lawyer who asked Jesus 'who is my neighbour?' was told an everyday story of a roadside mugging. Little did he know that it would require him to decide whether he would be a good neighbour or not!

As we enter the world of the parable we are challenged, drawn into making judgments about characters in the story, into making choices about whether we too will act as they did. A parable encourages us to believe that the key to our existence is hidden in the ordinary and that we ignore grasping hold of it at our peril.

Children at primary school sometimes ask whether assembly stories are true, by which they mean have they actually happened. And it is fair to ask whether we really need to take parables seriously, these stories which obviously do not recount historical events. The answer is that Jesus told these stories precisely to disturb his hearers' notions of what was true. We find it all too easy to skim information off the surface of life, about who said and did what, and to overlook the meaning of events. It is exactly that meaning which is captured in the art of story-telling. Parables often convey the mystery and demand of the kingdom of God far better than more ordinary ways of speaking.

Another good reason for listening to the parables is that it was Jesus who told them. The final truth of any story should be judged by the life of its teller. Does he live the truth he tells and does that truth liberate him and others? The answer in Christ's case is yes on both counts. For example, Jesus tells the story of a father who waits outside his home for the return of an ungrateful elder son; soon after, he himself is hanging on a cross, showing just the same patience even to an ungrateful thief. Jesus is the one who reveals the true God by what he says and does. He is 'the parable of God.'[8] So as well as listening to Jesus telling his parables we

---

8 Eduard Schweizer, *A Theological Introduction to the New Testament* (SPCK, 1991) p 140f.

shall also watch him travelling on the way he calls each of us to follow, towards Jerusalem, the place of destiny.

Two Parables to Cure Mammon Sickness

Jesus' parables offer a cure for Mammon sickness in two parts. First, as we shall see in the rest of this chapter, they show up the hidden choices we make against generosity and so open us to change. In the next chapter we shall see how parables also encourage us to step forward into a new world governed by a benevolent and generous Father. Rather than explain away these parables, I invite you to enter their world using the resources below.

The Parable of the Rich Farmer (12.15-21)

The situation—a bumper crop; the problem—what to do next?

- What words or phrases you would use to sum up the farmer's attitude? (If you are reading this in a group you can buzz with a neighbour.)
- You may have wanted to condemn the farmer's attitude, but how could the farmer have justified his decision to himself?

A key theme in this parable is the search for security. Governments today stand or fall on their ability to deliver a sense of security against threats such as crime and unemployment. In the parable the prospect of total security fixes the farmer's horizons. He decides to build larger barns, not just for his grain but for *everything*.

- You win £350,000 on the national lottery. What can you (and your family) now look forward to, providing you take sensible financial precautions? How do you feel about the prospect?
- Imagine you are in a supermarket which sells everything from lawn mowers to mouthwash to freeze-dried pheasant. Soothing music takes you gliding down the smooth aisles. You have all you could want and money to spare. You feel at home, surrounded by all these goods within your reach. *You are now enjoying the sort of life the farmer wanted to guarantee with his wealth.*

The rich farmer must decide what to do, but his decision is based on a misconception about how possessions and life are related. We are tempted to share in the same deceit by modern parables, which we know as advertisements.

- Draw a large triangle which points towards the top of a sheet of paper. This is going to become a picture of how important various goods are. Material goods, being the least important, go at the bottom of this triangle. Write down a few trivial examples along the base: you should have plenty of room for them. The more important a good is to human life the nearer it goes to the top of the triangle. As you go towards the top there is less room for choice. God, the ultimate Good, goes at the top.

- Put the following goods at the right level in the triangle (some can go on the same level): water, friendship, comfort, choice, hope, bread, salvation, health, popularity…and add a few of your own.

Few people believe that things are the most important goods, but many people can be persuaded that they will, in themselves, bring a higher good. You are not just buying an item, you are making a statement about your identity, winning certain appreciation from those you love, or even buying the hope that a coconut bar will give you a taste of Paradise!

- Think of an advertising slogan or image. For example, one car manufacturer in 1996 is comparing its cars to wombs. How does it persuade you that starting at the bottom of the triangle is the way towards the top?

The farmer has been foolish. He believes that *his* soul can be housed for many years in the store made by *his* barns, *his* grain and *his* goods. But his soul, the jewel in the crown of his possessions, turns out not to be his at all. It is required by God that night, and will be severed from the things which were supposed to give it life. And the possessions themselves, like Cinderella's magic coach, will turn back into mere things when the clock strikes the hour of his death. The spell of belonging will be broken and the barn become a soul-less shell.

- Reflect on Jesus' words to the people in the crowd: *Beware! Be on your guard against greed of every kind, for even when someone has more than enough, his possessions do not give him life…That is how it is with the man who piles up treasure for himself and remains a pauper in the sight of God.* (12.15, 21)

The choice the farmer had, and the choice we have, is *between anxiety and trust.* The one certainty we have about the future is that we are each going to die. We are mortal and with everything else we are passing away. Nothing created is eternal. And because we are mortal, things can hurt, harm, even kill us. We are not safe in this world: nothing can be trusted. So we are anxious. We will protect ourselves as we can.

Anxiety is not mentioned in the parable, though the farmer's foolishness consists in the fact that he tries to manage the impossible, to achieve ultimate security. The harvest need not have had an unhealthy effect on him, and barns (or storehouses) are not necessarily a bad thing.

- Read another story about storing grain in Genesis 41.46-57. Most of us try to save for the future, for instance in a savings account, life assurance or pension policy. Ask yourself how your own actions compare with both stories.

We need not be anxious because we are not alone. The Creator who sustains the natural order is at hand. We are his children whom he values and cares for above all else. What irony! The good harvest had been a sign of God's faithfulness, inviting the farmer to trust; but instead it opened the door to Mammon to feed on his anxiety. God is allowed no part in his reckoning, until God's voice intrudes on the farmer's inner dialogue.

To avoid being foolish ourselves we have to address the underlying problem of anxiety. Here are some heart-loosening exercises:

• Jesus' own advice is to consider the goodness of God in creation. Read Luke 12.22-31 slowly. Then read it again, this time stopping when you find a word or phrase that strikes you. Chew it over and let it take you into conversation with God your Father.
• Bring to mind a possession of yours which you hold dear. Ask yourself: what do I value about it? With whom can I share it? To whom would I give it? Could I do without it?
• How far do you agree with the saying, 'Happiness is not having what you want but wanting what you have'?

The Parable of Lazarus and the Rich Man (16.19-31)

No-one else is on the scene in the story of the rich farmer. But the next parable takes a split-screen approach. On one side of a gate a rich man feasting lavishly, on the other side a poor man, Lazarus, waiting in hope for a crumb from inside. The following meditation takes the gate's point of view:

I wish the dogs wouldn't do that—take advantage of Lazarus, poor beggar. His sores wouldn't make a snack for a gnat. What he could have done to deserve his luck I'll never know. The experts, they say he must have done something wrong, to bring down the Lord's displeasure upon him. I don't know. Poverty like that can't be an accident. But it just doesn't seem fair. With the Master on the other side, oblivious.

But he stays here, waiting and hoping. Waiting and hoping that one day— one fine day—the Master who built me to keep the likes of him out will pay him some attention, notice him on the way past, the rare occasion he ventures out, that is. Fat chance. He's sat there in his castle, surrounded by servants, surrounded by silk, surrounded by sumptuousness. The best that money can buy. Never in want. Always in plenty. Now there's someone who's been blessed, and very happy with it all to himself!

Ouch! What's happening to me. Excuse me, you can't do that. I was a gate not a...gulf. Nasty trick to play, even in a story. OK, where are we then. A few years on. I've been promoted...a barrier in heaven, would you believe! And I've lost my hinges, so now I can't let anyone in or out—'across,' I suppose I should say. And blimey, there's Lazarus! How did he get over there, with...Abraham. Of course I'd *heard* about him, being father of the nation. I never thought I'd actually *meet* him, and see him treating a beggar like he was a prince. That's a turnaround in anyone's books!

Do you mind! It's no use shouting. I am a *great* gulf, if I say so myself, and you are stuck on the wrong side. Yes, I can see that you are in torment, but it's no use...Oh, sorry, Master—I didn't recognize you without your silk and servants, and with that miserable look on your face. Well, yes, it is kind of rough on you—but I reckon it's only fair. Like Abraham says, you had your chances, so much time to change; but you never saw what you had to do. I just hope that your family realize how they might end up on the wrong side of a gate like me, if they use me to shut out the poor.

Now name your own and others' gates!
* Spend some time making a list of the ways that people are divided into 'us' and 'them,' so that 'we' can ignore 'their' need—suburb *v* slums, white *v* black...Then group you answers into different types of barrier.

The television continually brings images of the needy into our homes.
* Recall the last time you were watching a story which called for you to be generous. Was there something you wanted to do to help? What did you actually do? If you did not fulfil your original wish, what sort of inner gate got in the way?

In the first parable the hidden choice that the rich farmer faced was between anxiety and trust. The man's choice behind the gate is *between numbness and compassion*. Frighteningly, Mammon blinds him with the problem at his own doorstep. He has wealth enough to distract and protect him from the call that Lazarus's presence at his gate presents. He is disconnected from his neighbour.

Sometimes it is not physical wealth that numbs us.
* Read another of Jesus' parables (18.9ff). What is the Pharisee numbed by? From whom is he cut off?

* Reflect on Jesus' words to his disciples:
  Blessed are you who are in need;
  the kingdom of God is yours.
  Blessed are you who now grow hungry;
  you will be satisfied.
  Blessed are you who weep now;
  you will laugh...
  But alas for you who are rich;
  you have had your time of happiness.
  Alas for you who are well fed now;
  you will go hungry.
  Alas for you who laugh now;
  you will mourn and weep. (6.20-21, 24-25)

11

3

The Positive Side of Wealth

Two of Luke's parables have warned of the dangers of Mammon sickness, with its symptoms of anxiety and numbness. But Jesus' parables also teach us that personal wealth can also be a holy thing, if we invest it in the right way. In this chapter we shall discover some of the main benefits of wealth, using stories taken from everyday life, literature and Christian tradition. We shall go on looking at parables, but instead of taking them one at a time we shall select themes to point up these benefits.

Participation in Something Richer Than Me

Our culture has made us very aware of the self.[9] We live with a strong sense of a Me which seems to exist almost apart from others. We each imagine ourself as a unique and separate organism with an individual potential waiting to be realized.[10] Certainly this sense is not shared in other cultures where to be is to belong; but in our culture we live with a heightened and inward sense of self. This is where we have to start the Christian journey, and it is a precarious place; not far from the heightened sense of Me is a heightened sense of Mine which leads, as we saw in the first parable we studied, to the tragedy of a misplaced soul.

What a relief to know that the spiralling descent into self-absorption can be broken by generosity. As I write this, the World Snooker Championship is taking place. Occasionally, in a tight frame, a player manages to send the cue ball scuttling into the pack of reds to split the pack open. The character of the game is instantly changed, bringing the possibility of a big break. Generosity has a similar quality. It can redefine the way we relate to one another. Imagine a world in which people valued friendship more than things:

> Two elders who were living together in a cell had never had any disagreement. So one day one of them said to the other, 'Come on, let us have at least one quarrel, like other people.' The other answered, 'I don't know how to begin.' The first replied, 'I am going to put this brick between us, then I shall say, "It is mine." Then you have to say, "No, it belongs to me." That is what leads to strife and arguments.'
>
> So they placed the brick between them. One said, 'It is mine.' And the other, 'No. I am sure it belongs to me.' The first replied, 'It is not yours. It is mine.' Then the other cried, 'All right. If it belongs to you, take it!' And they did not succeed in quarrelling.[11]

---

9 See Robert Innes, *Personality Indicators and the Spiritual Life* (Grove Spirituality Series No 57, Cambridge: Grove Books, 1996).

10 Philip Sheldrake in *Spirituality and History* (SPCK, 1991) suggests that the power stemming from having material possessions gives us this feeling of autonomy.

11 Quoted in O Clement, *The Roots of Christian Mysticism* (New City, 1993) p 279.

In the kingdom of God we become aware that there is a higher value than Me and Mine, that wealth can be put to the service of a more lasting good. Wealth is not something that needs to be shunned but shared. This is the lesson of the parable of the unjust steward: 'So I say to you, use your worldly wealth[12] to make friends for yourselves, so that when money is a thing of the past you may be received into an eternal home' (16.9). My wealth can be something that contributes to the re-evaluation of my true self as I learn to share it and find solidarity with others.[13]

Solidarity is a strange word that sounds as if it belongs to the world of Polish trade unions or South American base communities. We might prefer the word friendship, which to our ears sounds warmer, more familiar and human. Unfortunately, it also conjures up images of a natural relationship based on shared likes and interests, whereas solidarity is a strange and quite unnatural bond which brings its own rewards, as the parable of the good Samaritan demonstrates (10.25-37).

The parable was told in response to a lawyer's question, 'Teacher what must I do to inherit eternal life?' So what does give life? The answer is neighbourliness, or solidarity. The priest and the Levite who go past on the other side of the road from the wounded man see him but see no connection with him. They go on, remaining in their own circle of business and imagination. We can imagine that once they reached their respective destinations and were among their own they would both be helpful and generous, as the Law required. But now they are on the way to their familiar world, not prepared to get involved. The Samaritan who lives as an outsider, on the other hand, can see the one on the outside as he is, and as belonging to his own, remote circle. He sees and goes up, bandages the man's wounds, bathes them with oil and wine, lifts him onto his own beast, brings him to an inn, and looks after him. Before he leaves he pays liberally for his upkeep, and promises not to abandon his responsibility as he goes on his way.

'Solidarity' is the graceful connection made between strangers by generosity. We admire the Samaritan for how his heart has room for others, and all the more because his compassion has wide and practical bounds which we know in our hearts could be ours, too, if only we were prepared to look beyond ourselves as we journey on life's way. So even if we dislike the word solidarity we must hold on to what it represents: a vision of a community created by overflowing generosity, in which we find our place by belonging to others. This is Luke's vision of church:

> The whole company of believers was united in heart and soul. Not one of them claimed any of his possessions as his own; everything was held in common. With great power the apostles bore witness to the resurrection of the Lord Jesus, and all were held in high esteem. There was never a needy person

---

12 Or unrighteous Mammon, a phrase current in first century Jewish terminology.
13 The Shared Interest Society (31 Mosley Street, Newcastle upon Tyne, NE1 1HX, 0191 261 5943) run accounts which enable investors to lend part of their savings in a generous but sensible fashion to groups of people in the Third World.

among them, because those who had property in land or houses would sell it, bring the proceeds of the sale, and lay them at the feet of the apostles, to be distributed to any who were in need. (Acts 4.32-35; cf 2.43-47)

Luke is holding up a mirror of the ideal to his Christian community, well aware of how, even in his time, the church had fallen far from grace. The tragic story of Ananias and Sapphira comes directly after this passage and shows how the rot began to set in, through resistance to the work of the Holy Spirit in the hearts of two disciples. This resistance is still present in us and still needs to be overcome for us to discover a freedom broader than ourselves. We have far greater resources than the early Christian community; what we lack is vision and motivation.

The priest and Levite in the parable of the good Samaritan were blinded to human need by their religious priorities; we are more often blinded by political and economic doctrines. Sadly, many believe more strongly in the power of market forces than in the Holy Spirit; and the deregulated market does not encourage consideration of the stranger. Its message is: 'Every competitor for him- or herself: we shall co-operate only if it is in our interest.' Nothing but this mentality could explain the reason given for a 12% cut over three years in the British Overseas Aid Budget, that certain needy nations had not achieved capitalism, democracy and self-improvement.[14] Generosity solely on our terms is no generosity at all: it is merely an exercise in national self-justification.

Luke wants us to realize that we have a choice to make between numbness and compassion, that we can choose compassion, and that if we do so we will be choosing life in the power of the Holy Spirit. In the rich one-third world Luke's portrait of the early church strikes us as an unrealized ideal and as a challenge which we usually resist; but for the two-thirds world it serves more like a blueprint for the joyful resistance of a community of the poor, who must share what they have in order to live. Christ calls those who live in plenty to open their gates and their eyes to share in something bigger than self-concern.

Meeting God in the Neighbour

We have travelled some way from a prison of Me and Mine; but what can be glimpsed on the horizon? We have seen that generosity is a way of making connections with others, but there is still more to say. Generosity is a path to God himself, who reveals himself in the neighbour. We have to be careful here of making two mistakes. The first is to start treating other people as a means of taking spiritual exercise, in other words, of using them as springboards to holiness. We may manage to convince ourselves that we are building interest in our spiritual bank account when in fact we are sharing the attitude of the Pharisee in Luke's parable (18.9-14), who did everything to satisfy his own sense of righteousness but in effect shut God out. As the parable tells us, his way of seeking God resulted in him praying to himself!

The other mistake, at the opposite extreme, is to disconnect loving God and

---

14 This was the reason given by David Shaw, MP in a Radio 4 interview.

loving your neighbour. This may not seem a likely error given the strong scriptural connection between the two (as in 10.27), but it is often done nonetheless. It becomes a danger whenever God is thought of as one object among others, a Someone whom you can only meet by going through certain narrow channels. Actually, our God is much more like a personal framework in which all other objects 'live and move and have their being' (Acts 17.28). A framework gives structure and meaning to all that is contained within it. God is not divorced from, or in competition with, anything else that he has created, particularly not with we human creatures whom he has made in his image.

God cannot to be pinned down to prescribed experiences but can be found at the horizon of any experience. Then the One who is present in the background comes to the foreground and discloses himself to us. Here is a personal example of the way God came close in an act of neighbourly generosity:

One day I was in town on the way to buy a birthday present for my wife. As I had just been to a church meeting I was, unusually, wearing a clerical collar. Suddenly I noticed a tall man in a shabby coat making tracks towards me. 'Oh no,' I thought, 'he's after money.' But it was too late to avoid him. 'Excuse me, Father. I'm not drunk.' He bent down and breathed heavily in my face while I held my breath. 'Could you buy me a cup of tea?'

He took me to a nearby cafe. I bought him a cup of tea, and a sandwich to demonstrate my generosity. We sat down on a bench outside watching the traffic streaming before us. He told me his name was David. 'What's yours?' 'Roland,' I said, not telling him what most people call me. We shook hands. David had been a security guard on the University campus where I now lived. He had been married then but his wife had left him when he started hearing voices. He was now quite a bit better, though he had never managed to hold down a job since.

'I won't keep you long, but when I've finished my tea will you pray for me?' I did. 'And who prays for you?' I admitted that very few people did face-to-face. David did. I don't remember what he said, though I knew that he meant it.

'Can I ask you a favour?'

'Yes,' I said.

'Can you give me a penny?'

'What do you want a penny for?'

'To make a phone call.'

'You'll need ten pence for that. Here, let me give you 10p.'

'No, I don't need 10p. I've got 9p already.'

I gave David the 10p bit and he poured his pennies into my hand. We shook hands again before we parted company, but the impression he made stayed with me. I had given him a snack and a penny and he had shown me dignity and human concern. It was a very unequal exchange. And I had the sense that in him God had drawn near and shown me my poverty.

Another story from the Christian tradition demonstrates the humble character and huge effect of generosity even more vividly:

> Martin of Tours was a Roman soldier. Riding on his horse one day he met a naked beggar. Slashing his cloak in two he shared it with him. That night he dreamt he saw Christ wearing half his cloak: 'This,' he said, 'was given to me by my servant Martin.'

Martin did not give away his whole cloak: it would have been easy to throw it down with a lordly gesture. But Martin shared his cloak and so met the beggar's need not only for warmth but also for a brother. Whenever we meet a needy stranger we have the choice of doing nothing (staying on our horse, hurrying on our way) and making our excuses or of stepping onto unfamiliar territory. If we open our arms to the world we shall not only find a sister or brother but also the hidden God who discloses himself in the neighbour, just as Lazarus could have been a gate for the rich man into the kingdom of God.

4

The Way to Generosity

Our journey is nearing its end. We now know that Luke's parables are like a mirror which we can hold up to our faces to see a world of hidden possibilities. But parables do more than give a vision of a coming kingdom: they form part of a gospel which invites us to step through the looking glass so that we become a parable of God. Luke has other stories to tell of real characters who find their human destiny amid the realities of life, people like the little tax collector up the tree, the widow in the temple and not least the son of Mary. Each of them has something to teach about a positive spirituality of generosity, one which is not just about what we do with our wallets, but about our willingness to give our whole selves more completely to one another and to God.[15]

A Spirituality of Relinquishment

Zaccheus has an itch (19.1-10). Nothing else can account for his extraordinary behaviour. A man who at his own people's expense has clawed his way to the top of his society finds himself shinnying up a tree to get a view of a passing Rabbi. Jesus looks up and calls him by name: 'Zaccheus, be quick and come down, for I must stay at your house today.' (Jesus uses 'must' to mean that in this way God's purpose will be fulfilled). Zaccheus has been scratched where he itches: 'Here and now, sir, I give half my possessions to charity; and if I have defrauded anyone, I will repay him four times over.' He has an honoured guest to welcome into his home; now is the time to make space in it for the salvation he brings.

The story of Zaccheus gives a proper perspective on giving. Not all are called to become materially poor. Some are: just before Zaccheus arrives on the scene a member of the ruling class comes to Jesus asking for eternal life (18.18-26). He keeps the Law but, as Jesus recognizes, he lacks one thing. So Christ tells him to sell everything he has and give to the poor, so that he will have treasure in heaven. Sadly, the ruler is not ready to change his heart's allegiance for the sake of the kingdom. We hear the fateful conclusion: 'When he heard this his heart sank, for he was a very rich man.' Zaccheus, on the other hand, bounds down from his tree and responds to Christ's call immediately and wholeheartedly. Everything he chooses to do with his wealth is intended to demonstrate his gratitude for Christ's acceptance of him: with the words 'Look, Lord,' Zaccheus begins his giving.[16] He has been freed from his attachment to his wealth so he is free to give plenty away in charity and in restitution.

---

15 Money is important because it represents the time, talents and energy we devote to our work and the personal power and opportunities we derive from our work. The offering of money in worship is therefore a highly symbolic act!

16 Here the NIV gives a more literal translation than the REB's 'here and now, sir' which stresses the concreteness and immediacy of Zaccheus's response.

17

Christian giving is founded on a renunciation of self and not of wealth. For some, like the rich young ruler and St Francis of Assisi, this has taken the form of a call to actual material poverty, but for all of us it is a call to change allegiance, from Mammon to God, to turn from all that pretends to offer life and instead to follow in Christ's way of liberation. Luke calls this change of lifestyle conversion, and with a change of heart it is possible. Rather than serving the demands of wealth, wealth can begin to serve us. We can use it to connect with our neighbour and to express our allegiance to God. We can begin to let go of our grip on wealth because we have another purse in which to invest, the kingdom of God (12.33).

Generosity which flows from a changed heart is unconditional. Giving with strings attached is not healthy, as we remain trapped by our possessions even as we give the appearance of being free from them.[17] As Jesus said to his disciples:

Treat others as you would like them to treat you. If you love only those who love you, what credit is that to you? Even sinners love those who love them. Again if you do good only to those who do good to you, what credit is there in that? Even sinners do as much. And if you lend only where you expect to be repaid, what credit is there in that? Even sinners lend to each other to be repaid in full. But you must love your enemies and do good, and lend without expecting any return; and you will have a rich reward. (6.31-35a)

Dostoevsky in *The Brothers Karamazov*[18] tells a wonderful tale which he in turn heard from a peasant woman:

Once upon a time there lived a horrid woman who was as wicked as could be, and she died. And she had not done a good deed in her life. The devils grabbed her and threw her into a burning lake. Her guardian angel was looking on and thought to himself: 'What good deed can I possibly recall to tell God about?' He remembered one, and said to God: 'She once,' he said, 'picked a spring onion from her garden and gave it to a beggar woman.' And God answered him: 'Why don't you,' he said, 'take this same onion, hold it out to her in the lake, and let her grab it and hold tight, and if you manage to pull her out of the lake, may she go to heaven, but if the onion breaks, may the old woman remain there.' The angel ran off to the woman and held out the onion to her: 'There you are, old woman,' he said, 'grab this and hold tight.' And he began to pull her out ever so carefully, and he had almost pulled her out when the other sinners in the lake, seeing that she was being rescued, began to cling to her so that they too might be pulled out. But the woman was as wicked as can be, and began to lash out with her feet: 'He's pulling me out, not you, it's my onion, not yours.' No sooner had she said this, than the onion snapped. And the woman fell back into the lake, where she's burning to this very day. And the angel burst into tears and left.

---

17 Needless to say, giving by Lottery, where the strings attached are the main attraction, can never be a form of Christian giving.
18 Trans. Ignat Avsey, *World's Classics*, (Oxford University Press, 1994) Bk 7.3.

The story of the spring onion highlights the problem but also the solution. If only the old woman could have given up the right to say 'mine' to her wealth and the power over others that went with it, then she would have escaped from the fiery lake. If we want to free ourselves from clinging to possessions we must renounce the selves that do the clinging, take responsibility for our destiny and follow Christ. This involves finding a new heart for ourselves with a new wholeness.

A Spirituality of Integrity

The story of the poor widow (21.1-4) illustrates another quality of Christian giving. This woman needs no encouragement to be generous.[19] Her heart is set on giving all that she has to the temple treasury. She has less than enough to live on, and yet she gives all that she can. Her sole intention is to give, which she does without show or flourish, unlike the rich who have a pious role to play out. All the money she has is pressed into the service of her one desire. And Jesus notices her—only he would have noticed her—because he has eyes to see a true generosity of heart which expresses itself in self-sacrifice.

Mammon has no part in this woman's life. She acts with one heart and mind. Jesus, we remember, has told us that we cannot serve God and Mammon (16.13). Our true loyalties will always end up with one or the other. If we serve Mammon we can still allow God an honorary place in our lives. He can be appointed as a prince of spiritual experience or religious devotion; but he cannot be worshipped as Lord and Master, on whom all depends and to whom all is directed. When Mammon says 'this is desirable' or 'that should be avoided' or 'this is not possible,' his will be the deciding word on the matter; and it will be up to faith to make the compromises. As long as someone serves Mammon that person will find generosity impossible.

Freedom comes slowly as we allow our faith to speak louder than those hidden scripts which tell us about the bottom line of life. We may barely recognize them, although we can come to sense them when we try to interrupt our inner dialogue with the words and pictures of the gospel. We look at Zaccheus or the widow and an inner voice says, 'You fool! How could you give all that up! That's all very well today, but think of tomorrow!' This struggle has to be faced honestly, and that is hard because it involves giving up the familiar self, the defended self, the self whom we believe is as much as we can be, and allowing ourselves to be formed around a new centre with a new integrity in Christ.

Susan handed her minister a cheque for £50 and asked if it was satisfactory. Her minister immediately replied, 'If it represents you.' Susan had been slightly upset by this comment and asked for her cheque back. The next day she returned to the minister with a cheque for £500 and asked if her gift was satisfactory. Her minister's reply was the same: 'If it represents you.' This time Susan had felt a deeper sense of distress and asked for her cheque back. Four days later, Susan returned to her minister and said, 'After hours of prayerful thought, I have come

---

19 She takes her place among a number of female givers in Luke's Gospel—see also 8.3.

to the conclusion that this gift does represent me and I am happy to give you a cheque for £5000.'[20]

The minister was wise to ask Susan to reconsider her gift without being concerned for the absolute amount. Susan's discipleship was deepened by his insistence, from an attempt to satisfy her minister to a search for integrity. She journeyed from seeking honour, through distress and questioning her motivation, till she found joy and a proper satisfaction that her gift was a true expression of her faithful self. In the end, her cheque represented the value she put on belonging to the church. It was a generous gift because it came from a new depth of awareness and a changed orientation in the self.

In the gospel passage quoted in the last section, Jesus promised those who learn to give generously a great reward. It continues: 'You will be sons of the Most High, because he himself is kind to the ungrateful and the wicked. Be compassionate as your Father is compassionate' (6.35b-36). Generosity gives a disciple a new identity, a sense that one is a shareholder in God's kingdom and that, by free grace, you belong to others and others to you. The generous self is less defended and more joyful than the modern average. And the generous also have the opportunity of seeing the real difference their giving can make to the world and to the church. Churches whose congregations have learnt generosity become effective signs of God's compassion. They become able and willing to resource reaching out to others, providing drop-in centres for the elderly, community workers, and educational support in schools, to give but a few examples.

The reward is great, but we flinch at the cost. Wealth can buy an individual instant and obvious gratification whereas generosity's reward is cumulative and less under our control. Money, in particular, gives an immediate sense of personal power; without it we have less freedom to consume and fewer options to play with. A disciple's freedom to choose must, in the end, be converted into a single choice for God.[21] So even if believers hear the word of God at first, they can be like seeds that fall among thistles: 'their growth is choked by cares and wealth and the pleasures of life' (8.14). Christians need a definitive and public parable which shows them the journey's end, the destiny that can be theirs with perseverance. The parable given is the cross of Christ.

A Spirituality of Trust

My experience is that becoming a more generous person is a slow and painful process: 'Jesus said, "It is easier for a camel to go through the eye of a needle than for a rich person to enter the kingdom of God." Those who heard asked, "Then who can be saved?" He answered, "What is impossible for men is possible for God."' (18.24-27). Growth is most likely whenever we become prepared to face things within ourselves and our circumstances which till then we had thought

---

20 I am grateful to Bishop Bill Flagg for this story, and for reminding me of the story of St Martin told in Chapter 3.
21 This theme is explored in Richard Bauckham's excellent booklet, *Freedom to Choose* (Grove Spirituality Series No 39, Nottingham: Grove Books, 1991).

fixed and given, and to put our excuses and guilty feelings under the light of faith.

Again and again I return to the crucifixion of Jesus (23.26-43), the point of his life when he seemed to have so little room for generosity and so much cause to be anxious and self-concerned. But he trusted his Father. The centurion who watched him dying testified, 'Beyond all doubt, this man was innocent' (23.47). This innocence was not about staying out of trouble (cf 22.37); rather, it was won by remaining in the Father's will and holding to his promises. Christ was able to be generous because he faced the limits on his life while holding to God's promises.

I want us to understand this generosity better. Luke is a story-teller and dramatist, and so we have to delve into his stories to discover his message. Luke is the only evangelist who tells us about the two thieves on either side of Christ and the events surrounding them (23.39-43). It is worth quoting the incident in full:

> One of the criminals hanging there taunted him: 'Are you not the Messiah? Save yourself, and us.' But the other rebuked him: 'Have you no fear of God? You are under the same sentence as he is. In our case it is plain justice; we are paying the price of our misdeeds. But this man has done nothing wrong.' And he said, 'Jesus, remember me when you come to your throne.' Jesus answered, 'Truly I tell you: today you will be with me in Paradise.'

At the end of his earthly ministry, as he was at its beginning (4.1-13), Jesus is tempted to use his power to justify himself and to secure his own safety. But he knows his mission and understands his destiny: he is passing over to the Father where he will enter into the glory promised to the Messiah.[22] As the penitent thief recognizes, what seems outwardly to be a failure worth scorning is in fact a supremely generous act endured for others. So he asks for a share in Christ's royal destiny. And Christ, the bearer of God's salvation, gives him that promise. The criminal's repentance brings an instant reward.

The cross challenges all who follow Christ but who feel no room to manoeuvre in 'real life.' The blockages we notice are usually outward limitations in our circumstances, but what prevents us from facing them generously is an inner poverty and insecurity hidden by unconscious habits of heart and mind. Often, like the thief who had done nothing to deserve salvation, we can only beg Christ to remember us in our stuckness. There is nothing we can do to save ourselves: all we can do is to bring as much as we know of ourselves and our circumstances to Christ, admitting that a lot of us does not want to change, and indeed, that we arrange our financial commitments so as to protect ourselves from change.

However, with persistence we can grow in grace and discover a greater personal freedom. Honestly admitting where we are is a first, but not the last, step on the way to generosity. The church today, as much as did Luke's community, needs

---

22 This is the likely meaning of 'Paradise' here; see J A Fitzmeyer, *Luke the Theologian: Aspects of his Teaching* (Geoffrey Chapman, 1989) p 209.

a longer range spirituality than a simple message of repentance, as it awaits the coming kingdom. We discover this from Christ's own consciousness, in his abiding sense of the close, compassionate and powerful presence of the Father who cared for each one of his children.

At his place of destiny Christ shows his followers the vital connection between generosity and trust. Because Christ trusts the Father without reserve he has no need for self-justification: he can give himself entirely to forgiveness (23.34). Because Christ trusts the Father without reserve he has no need for self-concern: he can attend to the particular needs of his neighbours (23.28, 43). Because Christ trusts the Father without reserve he has no need for any possession: he can give up even his spirit in sacrifice (23.46). Trust is what makes Christ a pure gift from the Father to all his children.

We are followers on the way of the cross, but we cannot step forward without our hearts finding a richness that they do not naturally possess. Our hearts cry out to be filled, but they cannot be satisfied with material things. What we need is a treasure to grow within us, out which we can give generously. The journey is difficult, but because of our own and not God's reluctance. As Christ promised: 'Would any father among you offer his son a snake when he asks for a fish, or a scorpion when he asks for an egg? If you, bad as you are, know how to give good things to your children, how much more will the heavenly Father give the Holy Spirit to those who ask him!' (11.11-13)

God is not reluctant to travel the road to generosity with us. But, in Luke's gospel, Christ puts a particular demand before us, that we should take up our cross daily and follow him. And daily discipleship means having to face often rather boring, ordinary and limiting circumstances with a practical trust in God:

> If in our daily life our mind
> be set to honour all we find,
> new treasures still, of countless price,
> God will provide for sacrifice.
>
> The trivial round, the common task,
> will give us all we ought to ask:
> room to deny ourselves, a road
> to bring us daily nearer God.[23]

As we draw nearer to God, step by small and obedient step, our eyes will grow to share Christ's vision of the Father's kingdom, and our lives become a parable of his overflowing generosity towards us.

---

23 John Keble, 1792-1866.

Appendix: Further Reading

Stephen Barton, *The Spirituality of the Gospels* (SPCK, 1992)
As the title implies this book interprets the spirituality of each of the four gospels. Barton brings out Luke's emphasis that spirituality is a response to grace involving joy, repentance and conversion to a new way of living.

St John Chrysostom, *Wealth and Poverty* (SVS Press, 1984)
Contains six sermons on the parable of the rich man and Lazarus given by perhaps the greatest of all preachers (Chrysostom means Golden-Mouthed), with an excellent introduction which summarizes the line of Chrysostom's thought.

Olivier Clement, *The Roots of Christian Mysticism* (New City, 1993)
The last chapter of this book describes how love of the neighbour grows under the impact of the Spirit. The whole book, though long, is a marvellous introductory reader in Orthodox theology.

Marie Dennis *et al*, *St Francis and the Foolishness of God* (Orbis, 1993)
A retelling of the life of St Francis that draws out its meaning for today. The first two chapters cover his encounter with the poor and his ongoing conversion. There are questions which provide an invitation to respond at the end of each chapter.

Richard Foster, *Money, Sex and Power* (Hodder and Stoughton, 1985)
A highly accessible book in which the author explores how money permeates all our personal relationships. It offers a practical spirituality of giving.

John C Haughey, *The Holy Use of Money: Personal Finances in the Light of Christian Faith* (Crossroad, 1986)
A detailed but fascinating study of the purpose of money, which argues that money should be used as the means of expressing our love for God. It pays particular attention to Luke's parables and to the problem of Mammon sickness. It laid the foundation for many of the ideas in this booklet.

Henri Nouwen, *The Return of the Prodigal Son* (DLT, 1992)
A lovely meditation on Rembrandt's picture of the parable, which invites the reader to take the part of each character in the story including the father's. A picture of the painting is included.

John V Taylor, *Enough is Enough* (SCM, 1975)
A classic study into the culture of consumerism but giving realistic ways for Christians to challenge it. The figures given in the book are unfortunately out of date, but not the very sensible theology.

Tony Walter, *All you Love is Need* (SPCK, 1985)

A book that exposes the way that the language of needs is used to justify how we behave in many different areas of life, including what we choose to buy.

David Wenham, *The Parables of Jesus: Pictures of Revolution* (Hodder and Stoughton, 1989)

This basic but perceptive survey of the parables sees them as pictures of the 'revolution of God,' a radical way that challenges the ideas and ideologies of Jesus' day and ours.